VERY IMPORTANT PEOPLE

LEWIS LATIMER

Engineering Wizard

DENISE LEWIS PATRICK

INTERIOR ILLUSTRATIONS BY
DANIEL DUNCAN

HARPER
An Imprint of HarperCollinsPublishers

For Jackson

Contents

Prologue

Young Lewis Latimer looked at his notes, then at the drawing on his desk. It had to be perfect. He knew he was very good at making detailed drawings for engineers and scientists. Would the man who hired him agree? He picked up his ruler to check his measurements once more. He was tired because he'd already worked a full day. But he was excited, too!

Not long ago, Lewis, an African American draftsman and office manager, had met Alexander Bell—a teacher of deaf students at a nearby school. They were almost the same age and they were both inventors in their spare time. Bell had heard about Latimer's drawing talent, and he needed it.

The newest invention Bell was working on might change the world. It was a machine that could send a human voice over a wire. Although most people in 1876 didn't believe the telephone could ever work, Latimer knew that Bell wasn't the only inventor with this idea. In fact, there was now a race to see who could get drawings and plans to the US Patent Office in Washington, DC, first! They were running out of time.

The clock ticked past ten as Lewis waited for Bell to arrive. If Bell approved the drawings, they'd be rushed to his lawyer and then to the patent office. Who would win the right to make telephones in America? Would it be Alexander Graham Bell, or the other inventor the newspapers talked about, Thomas Edison?

And what would any of it mean for the future of Lewis Howard Latimer—scientist, inventor, poet, artist, and the son of escaped slaves?

CHAPTER 1

Born in Freedom

Long before Lewis was born, his parents made a brave decision. On an October night in 1842, they ran away from the Virginia plantations where they had been enslaved people. George and Rebecca Latimer were ready to risk their lives to escape. It was worth it, they thought, to make sure that their children would be born free.

They hoped to get to Boston, Massachusetts—a city that had become a safe haven for runaways. In the Northern states there was a large free Black population and there were many abolitionists. Boston was nearly five hundred miles away, several days' travel on land and water.

George and Rebecca sneaked onto a ship in the port of Norfolk. It was headed for Baltimore, Maryland. They hid for nine hours, lying in the darkness below deck.

In Baltimore, George bought tickets to board another ship to Philadelphia. For that part of the journey he was able to disguise himself as a white gentleman because he was very light-skinned. Rebecca pretended to be his servant. Finally, after almost four days on the run, they arrived in Boston. But their dream of freedom quickly turned into a nightmare.

A man from Norfolk recognized George and contacted his owner, James Gray. Gray had put an advertisement in newspapers offering a fifty-dollar reward for his "Negro Man George." Rebecca's owner had done the same. Days after the Latimers set foot in Boston, George was arrested and charged with *larceny*, which actually meant he was accused of stealing himself!

$50 REWARD

RANAWAY on Monday night last my Negro Man George, commonly called. He is about 5 feet 3 or 4 inches high, about 22 years of age, his complexion a bright yellow, is of a compact well made frame, and is rather silent and slow spoken – I suspect that he went North Tuesday and will give Fifty Dollars reward and pay all necessary expenses if taken out of the State. Twenty Five Dollars reward will be given for his apprehension within the state.

The African American community was outraged. While Rebecca was taken to a secret hiding place in the city, almost three hundred Black men surrounded the courthouse where George was held, demanding that the authorities not release him to Gray.

William Lloyd Garrison

Frederick Douglass

Well-known abolitionist William Lloyd Garrison came to George's defense. Another group, calling itself the "Latimer Committee," even started a newspaper to report news about the case, the *Latimer Journal and North Star*. Frederick Douglass, who had escaped slavery himself and become a powerful speaker against the institution, got involved.

The Antislavery Movement

The first enslaved Africans were brought to America in 1619. By the late 1700s many Americans felt slavery was wrong and should be abolished, or ended for good.

Abolitionists spoke out against slavery in books and newspapers. They traveled across the country and around the world, giving speeches. The abolitionist movement included Northerners and Southerners, men and women, Black and white people.

There was a strong antislavery community in the Boston area. At the time the Latimers arrived, the New England Anti-Slavery Society had both Black and white members.

Many citizens began to demand new Massachusetts laws to protect runaway enslaved people. While George was being held in jail, James Gray came to town demanding the return of his "property." The *Latimer Journal and North Star* reported every bit of news to the public. After Gray went to the jail to try to get George to go back to Virginia with him, an editor interviewed George.

"I would rather die than go back," George told him.

Gray was surprised by the way people in Massachusetts supported the Latimers. As politicians worked to change the laws, Gray decided to sell George—for $400. Free African Americans and local abolitionists came up with the money. On November 17, 1842, a judge released George from jail and freed him from slavery. Meanwhile, more than sixty thousand people in Massachusetts added their names to a petition that abolitionists sent to their state government, asking them to ban the capture or arrest of fugitive slaves. The Latimer case changed Massachusetts law and became an example for similar court fights that followed. In March of 1843, state officials passed the Personal Liberty Act. Massachusetts had decided that no person could be captured as someone else's property and that every person had a right to be free.

George and Rebecca Latimer were now able to start their new life. Soon they became parents for the first time. They called their baby boy George, after his father. A few years later a daughter, Margaret, and another son, William, were born.

Finally came Lewis.

CHAPTER 2

Boyhood in Boston

Lewis Howard Latimer was born in 1848 in Chelsea, Massachusetts, across the Mystic River from Boston.

Not long after he was born his family moved back to Boston.

When Lewis started school, the Latimers were the only African Americans on their block. He and his brothers and sister had a hard time because white neighbors were not friendly to them or their parents. The family moved again and again, trying to find a place where they felt more welcome.

Finally, they settled in the West End of Boston, in an all–African American neighborhood. They stayed for many years.

When Lewis started school, his favorite subjects were reading, writing, music, and drawing. His teachers discovered that he was very smart, so they even let him skip a grade! Lewis liked keeping busy doing things. He helped out after school at his father's barbershop, sweeping up and keeping things neat.

Money was tight for the Latimer family, so Lewis's father took on a nighttime job hanging wallpaper. It wasn't unusual at that time for children to help their parents at work, or even to have real jobs of their own. Lewis went along, since he also enjoyed getting to spend time with his father. He put in the same effort and attention at work that he did in school, learning the paper-hanging trade so well by the time he was ten that he was almost as good at it as a grown-up!

His father also taught him how to paint houses, and he taught himself to make paper boxes for sale. Lewis's new skills earned money, so he stopped attending school to work with his father. For a time, they took jobs as paper hangers and house painters in the Boston area.

When Lewis was around ten, everything suddenly changed for the family. His father, George, abandoned them. Young Lewis never found out exactly what happened, or why.

The Fugitive Slave Laws

In 1850 America was becoming divided over slavery. The antislavery movement was growing, and like the Latimers, many enslaved people tried to escape to freedom. Abolitionists and others, including free Black people, were willing to hide and help them. But the US Congress passed new laws to help slave owners. Fugitive (runaway) slaves could be captured based on a slave owner's word, but had no legal right to speak in their own defense. People who refused to cooperate with the return of runaways could be fined and put in jail. Some historians think that Lewis's father, George, moved the family so many times and finally left them because he did not have any official papers to prove he was a free Black man. He may have been afraid that he or his wife might be recaptured and sent back into slavery.

What came next was something Lewis had never imagined. His mother, Rebecca, quickly realized that she couldn't earn enough money to support all four children by herself. Since Lewis was the youngest, she kept him at home. Margaret went to live with a family friend, and Lewis's teenage brothers, George and William, went to a place called the Farm School.

The Boston Farm School was one of many institutions across the country that trained children for work. It was located on an island four miles away from the city. Some of the children were orphans whose parents had died. Others, like the Latimers, had parents who could not afford to take care of them. The Farm School was only for boys, and it didn't accept children who had been in trouble of any kind. William was "bound out," or sent to work, to a nearby farmer. George went to work at a hotel.

For a while, Lewis continued to work to help his mother, delivering copies of the *Liberator*, a famous antislavery newspaper started by abolitionist William Lloyd Garrison. But when his mother got a job offer to work as a maid on a ship, she had to make another hard decision. She asked a judge to send Lewis to the Farm School, too.

Lewis *hated* it. He knew what his parents had gone through to live in freedom. He also knew, from reading the stories in the *Liberator*, that freedom still didn't exist for many enslaved people. Lewis didn't feel free at the Farm School. He wanted to go back home.

After he'd been there for some time, his brother William came back to the Farm School and found him. William wasn't happy where he was, either. So the boys made a plan—much like their parents had—to run away. They escaped one night, traveling with a white boy who also wanted badly to leave. It took several days of walking, begging, and sneaking food and rides on trains, but the boys made their way home!

Their surprised mother was happy to see them again and agreed to let them stay. She and Margaret were living together and working in Boston. Lewis knew that meant he had to find work to help make ends meet. There was no going back to school.

Lewis got a job at a lawyer's office, running errands. Later, he did odd jobs for a family. As the children struggled to help their mother, the country was struggling, too. On April 12, 1861—far away from Boston—shots were fired at Fort Sumter, South

Carolina. The War between the States, better known as the Civil War, had begun. Lewis was going on thirteen years old.

The Civil War and the issue of slavery divided the country and many families. But the Latimer brothers were united. They believed African Americans deserved freedom and equality. Lewis's oldest brother, George, volunteered with the Union Army's Twenty-Ninth Connecticut Regiment. A few weeks later, William joined the US Navy. Even though they were teenagers, George and William wanted a chance to prove themselves as soldiers, and as men.

Lewis wanted to be heroic, like them.

African American Soldiers in the Civil War

At the time the Civil War began, many Northern states had already outlawed slavery. However, Southern states had grown rich by using enslaved people to work in their cotton and tobacco fields. As the United States was growing westward, the Southern states wanted slavery to expand to the new western territories, too. The North and US President Abraham Lincoln were unwilling to accept the South's idea.

Many African Americans, both enslaved and free, wanted to join the Union cause. Harriet Tubman, an escaped slave, served as a spy for the Union Army. However, African American men were not officially able to fight for their own freedom until

Abraham Lincoln signed the Emancipation Proclamation, ending slavery, in 1862. Then, thousands of African Americans joined the US military. They went to battle wearing the blue uniforms of the Union like the Latimer boys did in 1863.

Some 180,000 African Americans served in the US Army during the war, and 18,000 served in the US Navy—most under white commanding officers. Army units from the United States Colored Troops (USCT) fought in Louisiana, Oklahoma, and Virginia. Several all-Black units became well known for their bravery, such as the Fifty-Fourth Massachusetts Volunteer Infantry. The courage of these soldiers began a tradition of military service for African Americans that continues today.

CHAPTER 3

A Boy Becomes a Man

Lewis was determined to help the North fight for freedom and liberty for African Americans. But the rules were that boys had to be at least eighteen years old to join the military. So just weeks after he turned sixteen, he lied about his age and enlisted in the Union Navy! He was assigned as a cabin boy to the warship USS *Massasoit*.

As a cabin boy, Lewis delivered orders from officers to crew members, carried messages, and did other chores aboard the ship. Later, he worked as a steward, helping to take care of the food supplies and meals. Life on the *Massasoit* was exciting and dangerous. As the ship sailed across the ocean,

there was always a chance they could be attacked. Luckily, Lewis made it back home safe and sound. When Lewis returned to Boston, he learned that his family had moved to Connecticut. Lewis wanted to stay in Boston. He had to figure out how to make it on his own. He desperately needed to find work.

The Union had won the war and slavery had been outlawed. But Lewis discovered that the great changes he'd expected as a result had not really happened. He thought that freedom for Black people would mean equal treatment, too. Jobs were scarce, and many simply weren't open to him because he was Black.

Even though Lewis was smart and a fast learner, he didn't have much luck. His mother came back to Boston and he moved in with her as he continued to look.

Finally, a family friend had good news. She worked in an office that was looking for a "colored" office boy "with a taste for drawing." Lewis jumped at the chance and was hired at a salary of three dollars (roughly sixteen dollars today) a week.

Once again, he was an office boy, cleaning and doing odd jobs. Crosby and Gould was a law firm that helped inventors protect their work. The company hired draftsmen to create careful, detailed drawings showing the parts of an invention and how it worked. When Lewis saw this, he believed he could learn this new type of drawing. He realized for the first time that his childhood love of drawing and painting could help him start a professional career. He began to imagine a totally new and different future for himself.

Lewis carefully watched the other draftsmen at their work. He observed the books and special tools they used. First, he went to the local library to try to find some of the same books. Then he had to save money to buy the supplies he needed, like paper and pens. Draftsmen also used special drafting instruments including a ruler, a compass, and a protractor. He went to second hand bookstores to find more books on mechanical drawing. With the help of one of the draftsmen, he improved his skills. And in his spare time at home, Lewis practiced and practiced.

When he felt his work was good enough, Lewis went to the boss and asked for a chance.

It was very unusual for an office boy—especially an African American one—to do such a thing. Many people believed African Americans were not as smart or capable as white people. They mistakenly thought Black people could never be successful in certain professions. But Lewis's fierce determination was part of what made him special.

What Is a Patent?

When an inventor comes up with a great idea to make or build something new, she may want to make sure no one can copy or steal that idea. In the United States, a **patent** is the legal way to protect her invention. A patent says that the invention is the property of the inventor. No one can make, use, or sell the same invention without breaking the laws of the United States.

To apply for a patent, the inventor has to submit written descriptions and drawings of the invention. She must also promise that she is the original creator. The US Patent Office looks over the application, and the process can take a year or more. The very first Patent Act was established in 1790 by President George Washington. A new Patent Act was passed in 1836. Since then over ten million patents have been granted!

At first, the boss only laughed at Lewis's request to become a draftsman. Then he gave him some paper and challenged Lewis to show what he could do. The man was so shocked at the quality of the drawings he saw that he agreed to allow Lewis to work on a few projects. Over time and through practice, Lewis got better and better. He was eventually hired to be a draftsman.

Outside of work, Lewis began writing, making up plays, and composing poetry. He kept up his art hobby, painting in watercolors and making charcoal drawings. He met and fell in love with a young woman named Mary Wilson. They married in 1873 and made a home in Boston. Mary encouraged Lewis's interest in science experiments and inventions.

Lewis was inspired by the world of patents and soon came up with an invention of his own. He created a design for a new and improved water closet (bathroom) for railroad trains. Working with a friend, Charles W. Brown, Lewis did the drawings. Together they applied for a patent. On February 10, 1874, they received a patent for "water-closets for railroad-cars." It was Lewis's first patent, but it wouldn't be his last.

Better, Faster, Safer: Other Nineteenth-Century Inventors

Despite the discrimination women and African Americans faced in their everyday lives during the late nineteenth century, many were not afraid to use the brains and talents they were born with to help push America ahead toward a new century.

Jan Matzeliger came to the United States from South America in 1873. He was part Dutch and part African. When he found a job with a shoemaker, shoe uppers were still being sewn to the soles by hand. People who had the skills to do this special work were called "hand lasters." They made good money—

and up to fifty pairs of shoes in a day. No one in the shoe business thought it possible for a machine to do the work, but after learning and studying the trade, Matzeliger invented one. He received a patent for it in 1883. His "lasting machine" could make up to seven hundred pairs of shoes in one day!

Granville T. Woods was born in Columbus, Ohio, in 1856. In many ways he was like Lewis Latimer, a smart African American boy who left school at ten years old and went to work to help his family. At his first job, he helped a machinist and learned to repair and build machines. Later, he went to night school. He became a fireman for a railroad company when he was only sixteen. He also worked at a steel mill and as an engineer on a British steamship. He started his own electrical company and invented many electrical and mechanical devices. Woods received more than fifty patents in his lifetime. He was sometimes called the "Black Edison."

Margaret Knight went to work in a cotton mill when she was just twelve years old. The work was hard and dangerous, especially for children. Knight's first invention was an improvement to one of the machines at the mill—when she was only thirteen! She never stopped creating and thinking. Years later, in 1871, she received her first patent. Knight had been working at a paper bag factory, where all the work was done by hand. She invented a machine to feed paper, cut it, and fold it to make more bags in less time. According to a New York Times newspaper story, in 1913 Margaret Knight was at work on her eighty-ninth invention.

Judy Reed and **Sarah Goode** may have been the first African American women to receive patents for their inventions. Not much is known about Reed, who in 1884 patented a "dough kneader and roller" for making bread. Goode owned a furniture store in Chicago. She received a patent in 1885 for a "cabinet bed," a bed that folded to form a desk.

CHAPTER 4

Lewis and the Revolution

Lewis taught himself to become an expert in the field of patent drawings. Within a few years, he became a supervisor at Crosby and Gould. At the same time that Lewis was rising in his career, another young man who was interested in the technology of the day had moved to Boston. He'd been born in Scotland and was teaching hearing-impaired students at the Boston School for the Deaf. His wife was also deaf.

Alexander Bell wanted to produce a device that would send the human voice over a wire by using electrical current. Although most people in 1876 didn't believe it could ever work, Bell wasn't the only inventor with this idea. In fact, there was now a race to see who could get drawings and plans to the US Patent Office in Washington, DC, first. Bell had heard about Lewis's drawing talent, and he needed it.

That's how Lewis found himself waiting at his desk one evening in 1876. He looked at his notes, then at the drawing on his desk. It had to be perfect, and he thought it was. But would Bell agree? Lewis picked up his ruler to check his measurements once more. He was tired because he'd already worked a full day. But he was excited, too.

Bell usually arrived after teaching day and night classes. He'd talk to Lewis about his device and give him instructions. They'd repeated this meeting routine over several weeks. Now the clock ticked past ten

as Lewis waited for Bell. If he approved the drawings, they'd be rushed to his lawyer and then to the patent office. They were running out of time. Who would win the right to make telephones in America? Would it be Alexander Graham Bell, or the other inventor the newspapers talked about, Thomas Edison?

As it turned out, Bell's patent was granted first, on March 7, 1876. At the time, neither Bell nor Latimer knew how important and indispensable the telephone would become. However, working with Bell gave Lewis an exciting new direction for his interest: the technology of electricity and electrical devices.

Lewis soon got a chance to explore this new technology at Crosby and Gould. He started making patent drawings for electrical railway signals. And as the field of electrical technology grew, Lewis studied every new discovery. He became more than a draftsman. He began to learn about patent law and the process of filing for patents. When a new partner, George Gregory, joined the firm, Lewis prepared legal documents for him.

But the two didn't get along, and after nearly eleven years, Lewis resigned from Crosby and Gregory. Finding another drafting position as an African American was very difficult. For a while he went back to his old job of hanging wallpaper. Although Lewis was glad to be working, it was a setback. He was proud of how far he'd come in the career he'd chosen, especially without schooling. He wanted to keep moving forward.

His sister, Margaret, wrote him with an idea: Why not move down to Bridgeport, Connecticut? She was married and living there. So were their brothers, George and William, and their mother.

Hoping for work that might allow him to combine his drafting and legal skills with his thirst for science and technology, Lewis and Mary decided to leave Boston. With the move to Bridgeport, the greatest adventures of Lewis Latimer's life and career were about to begin. He was about to become part of a *revolution*.

America Steams Ahead:
The Industrial Revolution

The race between inventors in Lewis Latimer's time was fierce and intense. Advances in science and technology were changing the way Americans worked and lived.

In the decades before the Civil War, most people lived on farms. Businesses were small, and it took many hours' work to make simple things like bread or shoes or clothes. The first big change came in the late 1790s and early 1800s. Two men, Samuel Slater from England and American Francis Cabot Lowell, invented machines to turn cotton plants into fabric. Their cotton mills did the work much faster than any humans could. The invention of the sewing machine by Elias Howe also sped up the process of making clothes.

Samuel Morse's telegraph made it easier for people to communicate—before, it took days or months for mail to be delivered from one place to another. And the discovery of steam power allowed boats to move people and packages up and down the country's rivers more easily than sails could. All of these inventions and discoveries sparked what's called the first Industrial Revolution.

More technology came about during the Civil War. The navy began using ships called **ironclads**. These boats were covered in iron or steel. They were able to survive gunfire better than wooden ones had. The first American submarine also changed the way wars were fought. Cameras and photography were new then, as well. In the 1860s, most people

 had never taken a picture or even seen a camera before. Mathew Brady and other photographers took pictures of soldiers on the battlefield. Their work showed people at home a powerful view of what war was really like.

Railroads already existed throughout much of the eastern part of the country, and they played a role in the war efforts. Trains moved soldiers and supplies on the battlefields more quickly than horses could. However, a second American Industrial Revolution seriously began when the cross-country, or **transcontinental**, railroad was completed in 1869. Instead of riding for months in bumpy stagecoaches or dusty wagons, people could travel from coast to coast in weeks.

New towns and cities sprang up along the way. And if Americans could travel faster, they wanted everything else in their lives to catch up! They wanted to talk to friends and family long-distance, instead of writing letters. Rather than light candles or turn on oil lamps, they wanted to flip a switch to turn on a lightbulb. For that, they needed electricity.

CHAPTER 5

The Spark of Electricity

Lewis quickly discovered that Bridgeport was "perfectly alive with inventors," as he wrote back to a Boston newspaper. Only a short time after he arrived in Connecticut, he gave a speech for the Bridgeport Scientific Society. Lewis shared his belief that there was creative power in both art and science. The group responded so well to Lewis's ideas that they made him a member. Though Lewis was happy to be accepted by other scientists, he was still looking for the type of work he wanted to do.

He found a job making pattern drawings for a local machine shop. One day while he was working, a man he didn't know came up to see what he was doing.

"I never saw a colored man making drawings!" the man said. Lewis talked about his experience in Boston. The man was interested. Lewis explained how he'd always loved art, and how once he discovered drafting, he'd taught himself this special type of drawing.

"I've been looking for a draftsman," the man told Lewis—and on the spot, he hired Lewis to be a draftsman and his personal assistant. The man was

Hiram Maxim, and he was the chief engineer of the US Electric Lighting Company.

Lewis began working for Maxim the very next week—and he was busy, which he loved! He was back in the world of electric technology. Hiram Maxim and other inventors around the world were in a race to perfect and patent the first *incandescent* lightbulb.

Lewis found out that Maxim's biggest rival was not far away, in New Jersey. He was the same

inventor who'd tried to beat out Alexander Graham Bell: Thomas Alva Edison.

At US Electric, Lewis had to catch up fast. In a short time, he had to learn everything he could about the operation and making of incandescent lights. He began working on the filament problem. Lewis met

the double challenges of learning about lighting and working for Maxim, who was a tough boss.

In the spring of 1880 Maxim's company moved to Brooklyn, New York, and Lewis went, too. He'd already become so knowledgeable that in addition to drafting, he was in charge of producing the carbon filaments for Maxim's lamps. He was actually working as an engineer. His duties included helping to make the lights during the day, as well as overseeing their installation at night in stores and offices across New York City. This work was much trickier—and more dangerous—than drawing.

Lewis once wrote, "These were strenuous times, and we made long hours each day." Installing and measuring electricity was a new science, and so were the tools and materials used by electrical engineers. Lewis later admitted that "a number of mysterious fires about this time were probably the fruit of our ignorance." Still, everyone wanted electric light, and US Lighting kept working to perfect its product. Lewis continued to experiment on his own to find ways to make lights safer.

He discovered that Hiram Maxim took credit for some of his employees' research. That didn't discourage Lewis. In 1881, he and Joseph V. Nichols received their own patent for creating a new way to connect the carbon filament in a lamp to the wires in its base.

In the meantime, Lewis kept working to improve on Edison's filament success. He invented a better way of treating filaments that kept them from breaking easily and allowed them to be molded into shapes. In 1882, he received a patent for the process. He sold the patent to Maxim. Later that same year Lewis patented his design for "Globe Supporter for Electric Lamps," and worked with Maxim to invent a new type of electric lamp.

About That Lightbulb . . .

At every step in the history of artificial light, many people worldwide were working on similar ideas at the same time. Gas light was introduced in England in the 1790s and gradually replaced the candles that people used to provide light in indoor spaces.

By the late 1800s, gas light was in use around the world for cooking and heating, too. Scientists and inventors were already on the hunt for cheaper, safer ways to provide light. They were on the trail of electricity.

The first type of electric light was the carbon arc lamp. The electric current traveled down one or two carbon rods into an open glass globe. These lights were very bright, perfect for street lights or large public spaces. But the rods had to be replaced often and the lamps were so hot they could cause fire hazards.

The race to improve on arc lighting was

intense. In England, Joseph Swan and St. George Lane-Fox were on the case. In the United States, in addition to Thomas Edison and Hiram Maxim, men such as Moses Farmer, William Sawyer, and Albon Man were all attempting to develop (and patent) the first incandescent lightbulb. Incandescent light was created by enclosing a **filament**, or very thin material, inside a glass bulb and heating the filament by sending electric current through it. The process wasn't easy. Too much air inside the bulb or the wrong filament material, such as those made of paper, would cause the lamp to burn out too quickly.

Edison's team developed a filament made of carbonized cotton sewing thread in 1879, and later one of bamboo that made his lightbulbs last nearly 1,200 hours!

Electric light was becoming popular in large spaces, too. Lewis designed and supervised the installation of electricity in several New York buildings and stores. He became an expert in outdoor light installations, so Maxim sent him to Philadelphia. His next assignment would take him out of the country for the first time! Lewis was sent to Montreal, Canada, to supervise installing incandescent and arc lights in the railroad station.

Lewis was confident that he could handle the job, but he did have one problem: Montreal was a French-speaking city, and his assistants there would speak French, too. Lewis only knew English. Once again, he used his ability to learn new things quickly.

He wrote a list of the work he needed done on the project and asked someone he knew to teach him how to give those orders in French.

In Montreal, he spent his days climbing telegraph poles at the work site and nights teaching himself French. Lewis wrote in his diary years later that the workers "seemed much impressed" that he tried so hard to speak and learn their language. The experience gave Lewis a lifelong thirst not only to improve his French, but to learn German and Greek, among other languages.

The Canadian job had taken Lewis away from Mary, and both looked forward to his returning home. When he did, Maxim promptly sent Lewis on another mission: this time to London, England, to set up an electrical lighting factory. When he boarded the ship to cross the Atlantic in the spring of 1882, Mary was with him.

It appeared to be a big advance in his career: Lewis was the only person at US Electrical Lighting who'd learned so much about every part of the light production business. And while he and Mary spent time exploring London together, the job proved to be harder than Lewis expected.

"My assistant and myself were in hot water from the first moment to the end of my engagement," he once wrote in his diary. Lewis had more difficulty giving instructions in that English-speaking country than he'd had in Montreal, although language

wasn't really the problem. There was a big difference between American and English ways of working, especially in the relationship between bosses and employees. Despite the conflicts, Lewis managed to get the factory up and running. By the time he was ready to head home after nine months, things had changed at US Electric Lighting Company.

Hiram Maxim had decided to leave the company. There was no longer any space, or any job, for Lewis.

CHAPTER 6

Edison's World

Although losing his position was disappointing, at the age of thirty-four Lewis had incredible experience with drafting, engineering, and patent law. He was able to find work, but competition in the growing electrical technology field was so fierce that many companies didn't last long.

While Lewis's work life was hard, his home life was happy. He and Mary became parents for the first time when daughter Emma Jeanette was born on June 12, 1883. They called her Jeanette. He was a devoted husband and father, buying gifts for her whenever he traveled. He wrote many letters and

poems to Mary.

Then one day in 1884, Lewis wrote in his diary, "The Edison people sent for me!" He had reached a high point in his career. Not once, but twice in his life great inventors had noticed his work and hired him.

When Lewis reported to the Edison Electric Light Company headquarters at 65 Fifth Avenue in New York City, he could barely contain his excitement!

Thomas Alva Edison

Perhaps no American inventor was so famous in his lifetime as Thomas Edison. Born in Ohio in 1847, he was mostly homeschooled. When he was still a boy, he sold newspapers on a railroad train and began making science experiments. He learned to use the telegraph, an early way of sending messages by wire, and worked in the Midwest as a teenage telegrapher. Edison's interest in communication led him to study electricity. He moved to Boston as a young man. By 1869 he moved to New York and began working on early inventions, including a fire alarm. He opened his own laboratories and hired scientists, researchers, and assistants from all over the world to help bring his awesome ideas to life.

Edison never stopped thinking or creating, and he was not satisfied by one or two successes! Over his career his inventions covered the fields of electric lighting and power, batteries, and home appliances like toasters. His lab in West Orange, New Jersey, had both a movie studio and a sound recording studio.

Edison made sound recordings and created phonographs (record players) to play them on. Even though most movies at the time were silent films, Edison was experimenting with adding sound. He even invented a talking doll!

In the United States alone, Edison received 1,093 patents for his inventions, and started 300 different companies. He died in 1931. Until the end of his life, he was full of curiosity and determination. Edison's contributions to science and the country were honored when his West Orange laboratory and home were named the Thomas Edison National Historical Park and opened to the public in 1962.

Lewis's first assignment for the Edison Company wasn't either drafting or supervising lamp production. He was sent traveling across the United States to speak to different electrical engineers and inventors about patents. He collected detailed information about the work they were doing in the field. Back in the home office, he worked in the engineering department, looking over drawings and models.

Just as in the earlier years of electrical technology, many people were working on similar ideas at the same time and attempting to be the first to

patent them. It wasn't unusual for some inventors to try to "borrow" another's design or work, which led to lawsuits. Lewis's background in patent law may have been why he was transferred to Edison's legal department around 1890.

There, he was in charge of the law library, and he did drawings for the lawyers to use as exhibits in court cases. Edison held hundreds of US patents, and numerous patents in countries around the world. His lawyers were often busy making sure others hadn't tried stealing Edison's designs or using any of

his patented work without permission. Occasionally Lewis traveled again, going to manufacturing plants across the United States to see if they were infringing on any Edison patents. He testified for the company in court cases about patents.

Sometimes European plants tried to use Edison's patents without permission, so in court Lewis often used the French and German that he'd taught himself long ago. His own experiments with lightbulb filaments helped win a case!

Lewis never worked side by side with Thomas Edison, but he came to Edison's attention for more than his knowledge inside the courtroom. Edison knew of Lewis's writing talents—Lewis sent Edison's assistant a copy of one of his poems in 1889. Lewis wondered if his work might be recorded at Edison's studio in New Jersey. (In addition to his work with electricity, Edison was experimenting with making phonographs and records. He often invited singers and musicians of the day to record in his studio in New Jersey.) In a letter to Lewis, the assistant said Edison thought the poem was "good." It's unclear if it was ever actually recorded, but Edison had another idea. He encouraged Lewis to write a book about electric lighting!

Lewis's 140-page book, *Incandescent Electric Lighting*, was published in 1890. It became popular among engineers and was used to teach students about lighting. The year 1890 was important for the Latimer family for another reason: Mary had their second daughter, Louise.

The years leading up to the turn of the twentieth century were filled with advances and changes in the electrical industry. The Edison Electric Light Company closed its legal department and merged with several other Edison companies to become the General Electric Company. And in the spring of 1896 General Electric and Westinghouse joined to form the Board of Patent Control. This organization helped solve problems with patent cases. Lewis's expertise and history helped him continue working despite these changes, and he became chief draftsman at the Board of Patent Control.

Throughout this time Lewis kept researching his

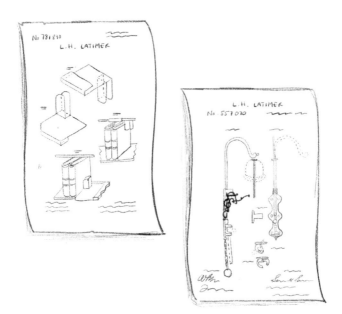

own ideas and creating new inventions. In 1886 he'd received a US patent for an early version of the air conditioner, and in 1896 his "locking rack for hats, coats, umbrellas, &c." was patented. Not long afterward he received his final patent for a "book supporter" in 1905. When the Board of Patent Control was disbanded in 1911, Lewis was sixty-three years old. But he wasn't ready to retire yet—from work, or from life.

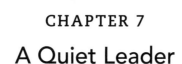

CHAPTER 7

A Quiet Leader

Lewis Latimer's achievements as an engineer and inventor had become well known by 1900. However, at the same time that he'd been exploring the limits of science and technology, he'd also been expanding the limits of people's thinking about how African American citizens could, and did, contribute to the country.

Amazingly, Frederick Douglass was still alive in 1894, and wrote to Lewis about having met his parents fifty-two years before. Douglass was a link to the injustice George and Rebecca Latimer had experienced in Boston. Because of his parents' experiences, Lewis was well aware of the injustices in his own time.

One of Lewis's main interests was improving the lives of other African Americans. He was a mentor to young people who were trying to start careers or get an education—like the son of a Haitian friend who came to the United States to attend the Pratt Institute in Brooklyn. On the local political scene, Lewis even wrote a letter of protest to New York mayor Seth Low in 1902 about the need for an African American member on the Brooklyn School Board. He also found time to keep in touch with many of the Black leaders of the day.

He read newspapers like the *New York Age*, an "Afro-American Journal of News and Opinion." He

regularly wrote to and received letters from Booker T. Washington, the founder of the Tuskegee Institute, an all-Black college in Alabama, and had W.E.B. Du Bois, a famous speaker and educator, as a visitor in his and Mary's home in Queens, New York.

Lewis knew well that education—from elementary school to college—was key in the fight for equality for everyone. During his free time, he began teaching English and drafting to immigrants at the Henry Street Settlement house in New York. He supported African American organizations such as the National Association of Colored Women and the National Conference of Colored Men. These groups and their members all across the country were part of the early civil rights movement.

Booker T. Washington and W.E.B. Du Bois

Booker Taliaferro Washington was born into slavery in Virginia in 1856. He was freed just before the end of the Civil War. In 1872 he walked to Hampton, Virginia, to attend the Hampton Institute. There, he grew to believe that it was important for African Americans to get both book learning and work training. After graduating, Washington became head of the Tuskegee Institute, an African American college in Alabama.

Meanwhile, as more African Americans worked to improve their lives with better education and jobs, racial discrimination was growing across the country. Some Black people wanted to leave the South altogether. Many were tired of waiting for equal rights. At the same time, many white people were not ready to treat them equally.

Washington felt that educated African Americans should stay in the South. He argued that it was better for them to work and contribute to their communities than to protest for change.

William Edward Burghardt Du Bois was more than ten years younger than Washington, born in 1868. He grew up in Massachusetts and attended both all-Black Fisk University

in Nashville, then Harvard University. He received a degree from Fisk in 1888, then three degrees from Harvard, in 1890, 1891, and 1895.

Du Bois studied social problems—and one of the biggest social problems he saw was racial discrimination. He felt that he "could not be a calm, cool, and detached scientist"  while African Americans had to live with unfair laws and violence. In Du Bois's 1903 book, *The Souls of Black Folk*, he argued that Booker T. Washington was wrong. He felt that Black equality could not, and should not, wait.

Washington and Du Bois were among the most well-known African American leaders of the early twentieth century. Although each had a different idea about the best way for Black people to become full and equal members of American society, both men cared deeply about improving the future of African Americans.

In a letter to the National Conference of Colored Men, Lewis clearly put the goals of thousands of African Americans into words: "I have faith to believe that the Nation will respond to our plea for equality before the law, security under the law, and an opportunity, by and through the maintenance of the law, to enjoy with our fellow citizens of all races and complexions the blessings guaranteed us under the Constitution, of 'life, liberty and the pursuit of happiness.'"

A different type of happiness came to the Latimer family in 1911, when their older daughter Jeanette married Gerald Norman, a young man from Jamaica. They settled near her parents and sister in Queens, New York. The Latimers enjoyed spending time together, going up to visit their Connecticut relatives or gathering on Sundays after church. All of them were musical, with Lewis playing flute and guitar, Jeanette on piano, and Mary and Louise singing. Jeanette and Gerald later had two children, Gerald and Winifred.

By 1918, although Lewis was having trouble with his eyesight, he was still working as a draftsman and engineering consultant with one of his old Edison coworkers, a patent lawyer named Edwin W. Hammer. That year, Lewis received what may have been the greatest honor of his career.

Edwin Hammer got the idea that the group of

men who'd worked for and directly with Thomas A. Edison should celebrate Edison's work and memory by coming together every year on his birthday. They formed a sort of club whose members were selected by invitation only. They called themselves the Edison Pioneers. The only African American among the twenty-eight charter (original) members was Lewis Howard Latimer. Lewis joined the group at the Edison laboratory in West Orange for a history-making photo.

Four years later, Lewis's failing eyesight caused him to retire. He continued to write poetry and letters and even studied Latin. Lewis's love of learning and creating was boundless! The year 1923 marked his and Mary's fiftieth wedding anniversary. The family hosted a big celebration. Friends and family sent hundreds of cards, telegrams, and letters to congratulate the couple.

Sadly, Mary became sick and died in 1924. Lewis was devastated. His daughters, Jeanette and Louise, wanted to cheer him up. They decided to put together many of the poems he'd written and had them published in a book as a seventy-seventh birthday gift. They called it *Poems of Love and Life*. Lewis never really recovered from Mary's death or the stroke he had afterward. Louise became his caregiver, giving up her job to do so. Her father died in his Queens, New York, house on December 11, 1928.

A Happy Life

There is nothing in this world,
'Mid its sorrow pain and strife,
That is sought for and fought for,
Much as a happy life.
It is everybody's longing,
It is everybody's wish,
And we aim at it, 'tho lame at it,
As the fisher strives for fish:
It is everybody's aim,
Every single soul's design,
To enjoy it, and employ it,
For the having it is fine.

—Lewis H. Latimer

Epilogue:
A Genius Shaped in Freedom

Lewis Howard Latimer's life was remarkable. He came into the world as the son of escaped slaves. After only a few years of school, he managed to accomplish incredible things in the world. He earned respect as a scientist, inventor, poet, artist, civil rights activist, father, husband, friend, and citizen.

In the years following the early breakthroughs of electrical engineering, Latimer's name was forgotten (or, possibly, ignored), but his genius is recognized today. Lewis never stopped learning. When he was challenged, he pushed himself to succeed. He floated through Alexander Bell's world and Thomas Edison's world, but he also created his own world.

As a Civil War veteran, he was a proud member of the Grand Army of the Republic (GAR), a Union Army veterans' organization. In Queens, New York, a public school and a housing community are named after him. There is even a Lewis H. Latimer House Museum, which is located in the house where Lewis lived, created, and laughed. Lewis H. Latimer can be forever remembered for light: the light his talents helped bring into the homes of millions, and the light *he* brought into the lives of those he knew.

Lewis Howard Latimer's Patents

1874 With Charles W. Brown: "Water-Closets for Railroad-Cars"

1881 With Joseph V. Nichols: "Electric Lamp"

1882 "Process of Manufacturing Carbons"

1882 With John Tregoning: "Globe Supporter for Electric Lamps"

1886 "Apparatus for Cooling and Disinfecting"

1896 "Locking Rack for Hats, Coats, Umbrellas, &c."

1905 "Book Supporter"

Timeline:
Lewis H. Latimer

1842
George and Rebecca
Latimer escape slavery
in Virginia; arrive in
Boston

1848
Lewis Howard Latimer
is born

1858
George Latimer leaves
the family; Lewis
leaves school

1873
Marries Mary Wilson

1874
Receives first US
patent

1876
Does patent drawings
for Alexander Graham
Bell's telephone

1864
Lewis volunteers for the navy to fight in the Civil War

1865
Lewis is honorably discharged from navy

1866-1878
Begins work as an office boy at the law firm of Crosby and Gould; teaches himself drafting; becomes head draftsman and office manager

1879
Moves to Bridgeport, CT

1880
Begins work at US Electric Lighting Company as draftsman and personal assistant to Hiram Maxim

1881
Travels to London, England, to start an incandescent light factory for US Electric Lighting

1882
Laid off from US Electric Lighting Company

1883–1885
Holds various jobs as draftsman and engineer

1889
Transferred to Edison Electric Light Company's legal department as draftsman and patents consultant

1890
Second daughter, Louise Rebecca, is born

1896
Board of Patent Control is created; Lewis serves as its chief draftsman

1924
Mary dies

1928
Lewis dies, December 11, 1928, in Flushing, New York

1883
First daughter, Emma
Jeanette, is born

1885
Hired by Edison
Electric Light Company
in New York

1911
Begins work in private
patent consulting firm
of Edwin Hammer

1918
Becomes charter
member of the Edison
Pioneers

1922
Retires from the
patent law firm
Hammer and
Schwartz

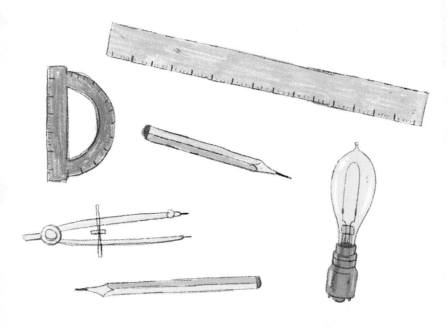

VIP Hall of Fame

Lewis Latimer helped pave the way for many other African American inventors. Here are a few modern-day creators whose clever inventions became popular:

Dr. Patricia Bath is a well-known ophthalmologist—a doctor who specializes in eye and vision care. She invented a laser-powered probe that helps blind people with a condition called cataracts see again.

Marie Van Brittan Brown was a nurse who codeveloped the first home security system. It was made of a motorized camera that could project images onto a TV monitor.

Lonnie G. Johnson is a former NASA engineer who invented the Super Soaker squirt gun. Johnson holds more than eighty patents, and twenty more are still pending.

Andre McCarter played in the NBA. In April 2000 he received a patent for his invention, the Touch Glove, which helps give athletes better control over a basketball when playing.

Bibliography

"Abolition, Anti-Slavery Movements, and the Rise of the Sectional Controversy." The African American Odyssey: A Quest for Full Citizenship. Library of Congress. 1998. "African Americans and the End of Slavery in Massachusetts." Massachusetts Historical Society. Accessed January 29, 2019. https://www.masshist.org/endofslavery/index.php.

"The Abolitionists." PBS Black Culture Connection. Accessed January 29, 2019.

http://www.pbs.org/wgbh/americanexperience/features/abolitionists-one-slave-makes-difference/.

http://www.pbs.org/wgbh/americanexperience/features/the-abolitionists-fugitive-slave-act/.

"Boston Abolitionists 1831–1865." Massachusetts Historical Society. Accessed January 29, 2019. https://www.masshist.org/features/boston-abolitionists.

"Civil War Facts." American Battlefield Trust. Accessed January 29, 2019. https://www.battlefields.org/learn/articles/civil-war-facts.

"Boy, Oh, Boys." USS Constitution Museum. October 2013. https://ussconstitutionmuseum.org/2013/10/09/boy-oh-boys.

Brooks, Rebecca Beatrice. "The Industrial Revolution in America." History of Massachusetts Blog. April 11, 2018. https://historyofmassachusetts.org/industrial-revolution-america.

Coddington, Ronald S. African American Faces of the Civil War: An Album. Baltimore: Johns Hopkins University Press, 2012.

"Competition to Edison's Lamp." Lighting a Revolution. Smithsonian National Museum of American History. Last updated May 2017. http://americanhistory.si.edu/lighting/19thcent/comp19.htm.

Edison Pioneers. Obituary of Lewis Howard Latimer, December 11, 1928. W. E. B. Du Bois Papers (MS 312). Special Collections and University Archives, University of Massachusetts Amherst Libraries. http://credo.library.umass.edu/view/full/mums312-b178-i618.

"Education of the Negro." Scottron, Samuel Raymond. *Brooklyn Daily Eagle*, January 26, 1901. Daniel Murray Pamphlet Collection, Library of Congress. https://www.loc.gov/item/72196273/.

The Faith Project. "Sojourner Truth." This Far by Faith. 2003. PBS. https://www.pbs.org/thisfarbyfaith/people/sojourner_truth.html.

French, Kimberly. "Black Inventor Helped Found Queens Church." *UU World*, October 30, 2006. https://www.uuworld.org/articles/latimer-african-american-inventor.

Fried, Joseph P. "A Campaign to Remember an Inventor." *New York Times*, August 6, 1988. https://nyti.ms/29szJp4.

"Granville T. Woods." Ohio History Central. Ohio History Connection. Accessed January 29, 2019. http://www.ohiohistorycentral.org/w/Granville_T._Woods.

Haskins, Jim. *Black Stars: African American Entrepreneurs*. New York: John Wiley and Sons, 1998. https://lccn.loc.gov/97037389.

"The Industrial Revolution in the United States: Teacher Guide." Teaching with Primary Sources. Library of Congress. Accessed January 29, 2019. http://www.loc.gov/teachers/

classroommaterials/primarysourcesets/industrial-revolution/
pdf/teacher_guide.pdf.

Kelly, Martin. "Significant Eras of the American Industrial Revolution."
ThoughtCo. Updated June 29, 2018. https://www.thoughtco.com/
significant-stages-american-industrial-revolution-4164132.

Kortemeier, Todd. *Unsung Heroes of Technology*. North Mankato, MN:
Peterson Publishing Company, 2017.

"Lewis H. Latimer: The Carbon-Filament Light Bulb." Lemelson-
MIT Program. Massachusetts Institute of Technology.
Accessed January 29, 2019. http://lemelson.mit.edu/resources/
lewis-h-latimer.

Lewis H. Latimer Papers, Winifred Latimer Norman Collection, and
Latimer Norman Family Collection. Latimer Family Papers.
Queens Public Library.

Matulka, Rebecca, and Daniel Wood. "The History of the Light Bulb."
US Department of Energy. November 22, 2013. https://www.
energy.gov/articles/history-light-bulb.

Norman, Winifred Latimer, and Lily Patterson. *Lewis Latimer,
Scientist*, Black Americans of Achievement. New York: Chelsea
House Publishers, 1994.

"Origins of Abolitionism." "I Will Be Heard!": Abolitionism in
America. Division of Rare and Manuscript Collections. Cornell
University Library. 2002. http://rmc.library.cornell.edu/
abolitionism/origins.htm.

"Picket Duty." The Civil War Day by Day. From Folder 14 in the John
McRae Papers #477, Southern Historical Collection, the Wilson

Library, University of North Carolina at Chapel Hill. Accessed January 29, 2019. https://blogs.lib.unc.edu/civilwar/index. php/2013/03/31/31-march-1863-2/.

Reidy, Joseph P. "Black Men in Navy Blue during the Civil War, Part 2." *Prologue* 33, no. 3 (Fall 2001). https://www.archives.gov/ publications/prologue/2001/fall/black-sailors-2.html.

Reimer, Terry. "Recruiting Exams and Disqualifications for Military Service." *Surgeon's Call*, November 9, 2002. http://www. civilwarmed.org/surgeons-call/exams.

Schneider, Janet M., and Bayla Singer, eds. *Blueprint for Change*. New York: Queens Borough Public Library, 1995. Exhibition catalog. http://edison.rutgers.edu/latimer/blueprnt.htm.

"Edison Pioneers Papers," biographical material. In Memoriam, Box 31. Edison National Historic Site Archives. Thomas Edison National Historical Park. US National Park Service.

"USPTO Recognizes Inventive Women during Women's History Month." United States Patent and Trademark Office. March 1, 2002. https://www.uspto.gov/about-us/news-updates/uspto-recognizes-inventive-women-during-womens-history-month.

"USS Massasoit." Historycentral. Accessed January 29, 2019. https:// www.historycentral.com/navy/gunboat/Massasoit.html.

"Incandescent Lighting: Edison Tech Center." http://edisontechcenter .org/incandescent.html.

Further Reading

For Students, Parents, and Teachers

On Lewis Latimer

Norman, Winifred Latimer, and Lily Patterson. *Lewis Latimer, Scientist*, Black Americans of Achievement. New York: Chelsea House Publishers, 1994.

Kortemeier, Todd. *Unsung Heroes of Technology*. North Mankato, MN: Peterson Publishing Company, 2017.

On the Industrial Revolution

"The Industrial Revolution in the United States: Teacher Guide." Teaching with Primary Sources. Library of Congress. Accessed January 29, 2019. http://www.loc.gov/teachers/classroommaterials/primarysourcesets/industrial-revolution/pdf/teacher_guide.pdf.

Acknowledgments

Special thanks to the Edison National Historical Site Archives and the Queens Public Library for use of the Lewis H. Latimer Papers, the Winifred Latimer Norman Collection, and the Latimer Norman Family Collection.

Acknowledgments

Special thanks to the Edison National Historical Site Archives and the Queens Public Library for use of the Lewis H. Latimer Papers, the Winifred Latimer Norman Collection, and the Latimer Norman Family Collection.

About the Author

Denise Lewis Patrick is a native of Natchitoches, Louisiana. She graduated with a BA in journalism from Northwestern State University of Louisiana and holds an MFA from the University of New Orleans.

She's written fiction and nonfiction for every age group, including board books, picture books, biographies, middle grade historical fiction, and young adult fiction. Her poetry has been published in several online literary magazines. She's volunteered as a mentor to young writers in a local after-school program and is currently an adjunct professor in the First-Year Writing Program at Montclair State University.

Her most recent works include the biography *A Girl Named Rosa*, the historical fiction novels *No Ordinary Sound* and *Never Stop Singing*, and the middle grade novel *Finding Someplace*.

In her spare time, she writes poetry and makes cloth dolls. She is also the married mother of adult sons.